meals
on the go
quick & easy recipes for active families

meals
on the go
quick & easy recipes for active families

meals
on the go
quick & easy recipes for active families

Publications International, Ltd.

Favorite Brand Name Recipes at www.fbnr.com

Pictured on the front cover *(clockwise from top left):* Pizza Snack Cups *(page 64),* Take-Along Snack Mix *(page 74),* Rainbow Spirals *(page 44),* Quick & Easy Meatball Soup *(page 42),* Dizzy Dogs *(page 52)* and Golden Chicken Nuggets *(page 52).*

Pictured on the back cover *(clockwise from top left):* Best Ever Hero Sandwich *(page 46),* Snacking Surprise Muffins *(page 70),* 3-Cheese Chicken & Noodles *(page 80)* and Breakfast Pizza *(page 18).*

ISBN-13: 978-1-4127-2681-8
ISBN-10: 1-4127-2681-6

Manufactured in China.

8 7 6 5 4 3 2 1

Microwave Cooking: Microwave ovens vary in wattage. Use the cooking times as guidelines and check for doneness before adding more time.

Preparation/Cooking Times: Preparation times are based on the approximate amount of time required to assemble the recipe before cooking, baking, chilling or serving. These times include preparation steps such as measuring, chopping and mixing. The fact that some preparations and cooking can be done simultaneously is taken into account. Preparation of optional ingredients and serving suggestions is not included.

table of contents

on-the-go guide
to good eating

Whether you're chauffeuring the soccer team to practice, driving the daily car pool, rushing to catch the commuter express, packing another lunch—or simply running late—you're probably wishing there were easier, healthier and more appealing ways to eat on the go. Now there are!

Inside you'll discover dozens of creative ideas for making nutritious breakfasts, satisfying lunches and hearty meals that travel well and keep everyone well fed. Plus, you'll find a carload of new recipes for portable snacks that offer an energy boost either on the field, on the job or on the run. For busy weeknights, we've included family-friendly slow cooker recipes, so dinner's hot, flavorful and ready to serve when you walk in the door.

Here are a few tips to help you get the most "mileage" from *Food on the Go!*

keep it colorful
No matter *where* you eat, you eat with your eyes as well as your tastebuds. Make portable food more colorful and appetizing by adding brightly colored fruits and vegetables. Not only do they make the meal more appealing, they also provide extra nutritional benefits.

go for variety
Eating on the go doesn't have to be boring. Use the opportunity to broaden your horizons and try new foods and recipes. By eating a wider variety of foods, you'll improve your chances of eating a balanced diet that fuels your entire body.

play it safe
Keep hot food hot (140°F or above) and cold food cold (40°F or below). To keep food cool, use an insulated bag with a frozen ice pack or freeze a drink box or plastic drink bottle overnight and pack it in with the food. Carry hot food in a thermos or insulated bag.

think small
Fresh fruits and vegetables, sandwiches, snacks and even desserts are easier to handle if they are cut into bite-sized pieces or easy-to-manage finger food. They're also a lot more fun!

brown bag benefits

Home-packed lunches, meals, and snacks offer a cheaper and usually healthier alternative to school food, fast food and vending machines. They

can be customized to fit individual preferences and provide more variety. In short, they give you more control over what you and your family are eating.

pack it up

Be creative when packing portable food. Think outside the box:

- plastic bowls, cups and containers with lids
- waxed paper, foil, plastic wrap, freezer and butcher paper
- plastic bags, waxed paper bags and cellophane bags with twist ties
- thermoses for both hot and cold foods
- paper drinking cups
- small cardboard boxes
- rinsed-out vitamin bottles for condiments
- recycled baby food jars
- washed yogurt, cottage cheese and margarine containers
- wicker baskets
- children's beach pails
- empty oatmeal or cornmeal cartons
- produce baskets
- food used as edible bowls: melon halves, bell pepper cups

backseat
breakfasts

Breakfast in a Cup
Makes 12 servings

> **3 cups cooked rice**
> **1 cup (4 ounces) shredded Cheddar cheese, divided**
> **1 can (4 ounces) diced green chilies**
> **1 jar (2 ounces) diced pimientos, drained**
> **⅓ cup skim milk**
> **2 eggs, beaten**
> **½ teaspoon ground cumin**
> **½ teaspoon salt**
> **½ teaspoon ground black pepper**
> **Vegetable cooking spray**

Combine rice, ½ cup cheese, chilies, pimientos, milk, eggs, cumin, salt and pepper in large bowl. Evenly divide mixture into 12 muffin cups coated with cooking spray. Sprinkle with remaining ½ cup cheese. Bake at 400°F. for 15 minutes or until set.

Tip: Breakfast cups may be stored in the freezer in a freezer bag or tightly sealed container. To reheat frozen breakfast cups, microwave each cup on HIGH 1 minute.

*Favorite recipe from **USA Rice Federation***

Breakfast in a Cup

Sausage Pinwheels

Makes 48 pinwheels

2 cups biscuit mix
½ cup milk
¼ cup butter or margarine, melted
1 pound BOB EVANS® Original Recipe Roll Sausage

Combine biscuit mix, milk and butter in large bowl until blended. Refrigerate 30 minutes. Divide dough into two portions. Roll out one portion on floured surface to ⅛-inch-thick rectangle, about 10×7 inches. Spread with half the sausage. Roll lengthwise into long roll. Repeat with remaining dough and sausage. Place rolls in freezer until hard enough to cut easily. Preheat oven to 400°F. Cut rolls into thin slices. Place on baking sheets. Bake 15 minutes or until golden brown. Serve hot. Refrigerate leftovers.

Note: This recipe may be doubled. Refreeze after slicing. When ready to serve, thaw slices in refrigerator and bake.

Triple Berry Breakfast Parfait

Makes 4 servings

2 cups vanilla sugar-free nonfat yogurt
¼ teaspoon ground cinnamon
1 cup sliced strawberries
½ cup blueberries
½ cup raspberries
1 cup low-fat granola without raisins

1. Combine yogurt and cinnamon in small bowl. Combine strawberries, blueberries and raspberries in medium bowl.

2. For each parfait, layer ¼ cup fruit mixture, 2 tablespoons granola and ¼ cup yogurt mixture in parfait glass; repeat layers. Garnish with mint leaves, if desired.

Sausage Pinwheels

Spanish Omelet

Makes 6 servings

> **8 large eggs, beaten**
> **3 cups (16 ounces) frozen cubed or shredded hash brown potatoes**
> **1½ cups *French's*® French Fried Onions**
> **Salsa**
> ***Frank's*® RedHot® Original Cayenne Pepper Sauce**

1. Beat eggs with ½ *teaspoon salt* and ¼ *teaspoon pepper* in large bowl; set aside.

2. Heat *2 tablespoons oil* until very hot in 10-inch nonstick oven-safe skillet over medium-high heat. Sauté potatoes about 7 minutes or until browned, stirring often.

3. Stir ½ *cup* French Fried Onions and beaten eggs into potato mixture. Cook, uncovered, over low heat 15 minutes or until eggs are almost set. *Do not stir*. Sprinkle eggs with remaining *1 cup* onions. Cover and cook 8 minutes or until eggs are fully set. Cut into wedges and serve with salsa. Splash on ***Frank's RedHot*** Sauce to taste.

Prep Time: 5 minutes
Cook Time: 30 minutes

Fruit 'n Juice Breakfast Shake

Makes 2 servings

> **1 extra-ripe, medium DOLE® Banana**
> **¾ cup DOLE® Pineapple Juice**
> **½ cup lowfat vanilla yogurt**
> **½ cup blueberries**

Combine all ingredients in blender. Process until smooth.

Spanish Omelet

Ham and Cheese Corn Muffins

Makes 9 muffins

1 package (about 8 ounces) corn muffin mix
½ cup chopped deli ham
½ cup (2 ounces) shredded Swiss cheese
⅓ cup reduced-fat (2%) milk
1 egg
1 tablespoon Dijon mustard

1. Preheat oven to 400°F. Combine muffin mix, ham and cheese in medium bowl.

2. Combine milk, egg and mustard in 1-cup glass measure. Stir milk mixture into dry ingredients; mix just until moistened.

3. Fill 9 paper cup-lined 2¾-inch muffin cups two-thirds full with batter.

4. Bake 18 to 20 minutes or until light golden brown. Remove muffin pan to cooling rack. Let stand 5 minutes. Serve warm.

Prep and Cook Time: 30 minutes

Serving Suggestion: For added flavor, serve Ham and Cheese Corn Muffins with honey-flavored butter. To prepare, stir together equal amounts of honey and softened butter.

Sunrise Squares

Makes 6 servings

1 pound BOB EVANS® Original Recipe Roll Sausage
2 slices bread, cut into ½-inch cubes (about 2 cups)
1 cup (4 ounces) shredded sharp Cheddar cheese
6 eggs
2 cups milk
½ teaspoon salt
½ teaspoon dry mustard

Preheat oven to 350°F. Crumble sausage into medium skillet. Cook over medium heat until browned, stirring occasionally. Drain off any drippings. Spread bread cubes in greased 11×7-inch baking dish; top with sausage and cheese. Whisk eggs, milk, salt and mustard until well blended; pour over cheese. Bake 30 to 40 minutes or until set. Let stand 5 minutes before cutting into squares; serve hot. Refrigerate leftovers.

Tip: You can make this tasty meal ahead and refrigerate overnight before baking.

Ham and Cheese Corn Muffins

Peanut Butter and Jelly Pizza Sandwich

Makes 1 serving

> **1 English muffin**
> **2 tablespoons JIF® Creamy Peanut Butter**
> **2 tablespoons SMUCKER'S® Strawberry Jam**
> **8 slices banana**
>   **Chocolate syrup**
>   **Sweetened, flaked coconut (optional)**

1. Split and toast English muffin. Spread JIF® peanut butter on both sides of the English muffin. Spread SMUCKER'S® Strawberry Jam on JIF® peanut butter.

2. Top with banana slices. Drizzle on chocolate syrup to taste. Sprinkle coconut flakes if desired. Eat while still warm.

Hawaiian Breakfast Wrap

Makes 4 servings

> **6 eggs**
> **¼ cup milk or water**
> **¼ cup chopped ham**
> **¼ cup chopped DOLE® Red or Green Bell Pepper**
> **2 tablespoons margarine**
> **1 can (8 ounces) DOLE® Crushed Pineapple, drained**
> **4 (8-inch) flour tortillas**

• Beat together eggs and milk in medium bowl until blended. Set aside.

• Cook ham and bell pepper in hot margarine over medium heat in large skillet until ham is lightly browned and vegetables are tender-crisp. Stir in egg mixture and crushed pineapple. Scramble until desired doneness, stirring constantly.

• Evenly divide egg mixture onto flour tortillas. Roll sides up. Serve with watermelon wedges and lime slice, if desired. Serve immediately.

Prep Time: 15 minutes

Peanut Butter and Jelly Pizza Sandwich

Breakfast Pizza

Makes 6 servings

> 1 can (10 ounces) refrigerated biscuit dough
> ½ pound bacon slices
> 2 tablespoons butter or margarine
> 2 tablespoons all-purpose flour
> ¼ teaspoon salt
> ⅛ teaspoon black pepper
> 1½ cups milk
> ½ cup (2 ounces) shredded sharp Cheddar cheese
> ¼ cup sliced green onions
> ¼ cup chopped red bell pepper

Preheat oven to 350°F. Spray 13×9-inch baking dish with nonstick cooking spray.

Separate biscuit dough and arrange in rectangle on lightly floured surface. Roll into 14×10-inch rectangle. Place in prepared dish; pat edges up sides of dish. Bake 15 minutes. Remove from oven and set aside.

Meanwhile, place bacon in single layer in large skillet; cook over medium heat until crisp. Remove from skillet; drain on paper towels. Crumble and set aside.

Melt butter in medium saucepan over medium heat. Stir in flour, salt and black pepper until smooth. Gradually stir in milk; cook and stir until thickened. Stir in cheese until melted. Spread sauce evenly over baked crust. Arrange bacon, green onions and bell pepper over sauce.

Bake, uncovered, 20 minutes or until crust is golden brown.

On-the-Go Guide

Research shows that eating breakfast improves concentration, thinking and problem solving. With portable foods like these on hand, there's no excuse for kids—or parents—to miss the most important meal of the day. Add a carton of orange juice or a piece of fruit to round out the meal.

Breakfast Pizza

goodies
to go

Gingerbread Squares
Makes 9 servings

   3 tablespoons margarine, softened
   2 tablespoons light brown sugar
   ¼ cup molasses
   1 egg white
1¼ cups all-purpose flour
   ½ teaspoon baking soda
   ½ teaspoon ground ginger
   ½ teaspoon ground cinnamon
   ¼ teaspoon salt
   1 cup sweetened applesauce
     Decorations: tube frostings, colored sugars, red hot
       cinnamon candies or other small candies (optional)

1. Preheat oven to 350°F. Spray 8-inch square baking pan with nonstick cooking spray; set aside.

2. Combine margarine and sugar with wooden spoon in medium bowl until well blended. Beat in molasses and egg white.

3. Combine dry ingredients in small bowl; mix well. Add to margarine mixture alternately with applesauce, mixing well after each addition. Transfer batter to prepared pan.

4. Bake 25 to 30 minutes or until toothpick inserted into center comes out clean. Cool completely on wire rack. Cut into squares. Frost and decorate, if desired.

Gingerbread Squares

Tooty Fruitys

Makes 10 servings

> 1 package (10 ounces) extra-light flaky biscuits
> 10 (1½-inch) fruit pieces, such as plum, apple, peach or pear
> 1 egg white
> 1 teaspoon water
>   Powdered sugar (optional)

1. Preheat oven to 425°F. Spray baking sheets with nonstick cooking spray; set aside.

2. Separate biscuits. Place on lightly floured surface. Roll with lightly floured rolling pin or flatten dough with fingers to form 3½-inch circles. Place 1 fruit piece in center of each circle. Bring 3 edges of dough up over fruit; pinch edges together to seal. Place on prepared baking sheet.

3. Beat egg white with water in small bowl; brush over dough.

4. Bake until golden brown, 10 to 15 minutes. Remove to wire rack to cool. Serve warm or at room temperature. Sprinkle with powdered sugar, if desired, just before serving.

Sweet Tooty Fruitys: Prepare dough circles as directed. Gently press both sides of dough circles into granulated or cinnamon-sugar to coat completely. Top with fruit and continue as directed, except do not brush with egg white mixture or sprinkle with powdered sugar.

Cheesy Tooty Fruitys: Prepare dough circles as directed. Top each circle with ½ teaspoon softened reduced-fat cream cheese in addition to the fruit. Continue as directed.

On-the-Go Guide

What a great way to disguise fruit! This recipe will make even nonfruit lovers want to grab these tasty treats on their way out.

Tooty Fruitys

No-Bake Cherry Crisps

Makes about 3 dozen cookies

¼ **cup butter, softened**
1 **cup powdered sugar**
1 **cup peanut butter**
1⅓ **cups crisp rice cereal**
½ **cup maraschino cherries, drained, dried and chopped**
¼ **cup plus 2 tablespoons mini semisweet chocolate chips**
¼ **cup chopped pecans**
1 to 2 **cups flaked coconut (for rolling)**

Beat butter, powdered sugar and peanut butter in large bowl. Stir in cereal, cherries, chocolate chips and pecans. Mix well. Shape teaspoonfuls of dough into 1-inch balls. Roll in coconut. Place on cookie sheets and refrigerate 1 hour. Store in refrigerator.

Waikiki Cookies

Makes about 3 dozen cookies

1½ **cups packed light brown sugar**
⅔ **cups shortening**
1 **tablespoon water**
1 **teaspoon vanilla**
2 **eggs**
1¾ **cups all-purpose flour**
½ **teaspoon salt**
¼ **teaspoon baking soda**
1 **cup white chocolate chunks**
1 **cup macadamia nuts, coarsely chopped**

1. Preheat oven to 375°F.

2. Combine brown sugar, shortening, water and vanilla in large bowl. Beat at medium speed of electric mixer until well blended. Add eggs; beat well.

3. Combine flour, salt and baking soda in medium bowl. Add to sugar mixture; beat at low speed just until blended. Stir in white chocolate chunks and nuts.

4. Drop dough by rounded tablespoonfuls 2 inches apart onto ungreased baking sheet.

5. Bake 7 to 9 minutes or until cookies are set. Do not overbake. Cool 2 minutes on baking sheet. Remove cookies to wire rack; cool completely.

No-Bake Cherry Crisps

Lollipop Sugar Cookies

Makes about 3 dozen cookies

- 1¼ **cups granulated sugar**
- 1 **cup Butter Flavor CRISCO® all-vegetable shortening**
  or 1 Butter Flavor CRISCO® Stick
- 2 **eggs**
- ¼ **cup light corn syrup or regular pancake syrup**
- 1 **tablespoon vanilla**
- 3 **cups all-purpose flour**
- ¾ **teaspoon baking powder**
- ½ **teaspoon baking soda**
- ½ **teaspoon salt**
- 36 **flat ice cream sticks**
  Any of the following: miniature baking chips, raisins,
  red hots, nonpareils, colored sugar or nuts

1. Combine sugar and 1 cup shortening in large bowl. Beat at medium speed of electric mixer until well blended. Add eggs, syrup and vanilla; beat until well blended and fluffy.

2. Combine flour, baking powder, baking soda and salt. Add gradually to creamed mixture at low speed until well blended. Wrap dough in plastic wrap. Refrigerate at least 1 hour.

3. Heat oven to 375°F. Place foil on countertop for cooling cookies.

4. Shape dough into 1½-inch balls. Push ice cream stick into center of each ball. Place balls 3 inches apart on ungreased baking sheet. Flatten balls to ½-inch thickness with bottom of greased and floured glass. Decorate as desired; press decorations gently into dough.*

5. Bake at 375°F for 8 to 10 minutes. *Do not overbake.* Cool on baking sheet 2 minutes. Remove cookies to foil to cool completely.

*Cookies can also be painted before baking. Mix 1 egg yolk and ¼ teaspoon water. Divide into 3 small cups. Add 2 to 3 drops food color to each. Stir. Use clean water color brushes to paint designs on cookies.

Lollipop Sugar Cookies

goodies **to go**

Bread Pudding Snacks

Makes 12 servings

1¼ cups reduced-fat (2%) milk
½ cup cholesterol-free egg substitute
⅓ cup sugar
1 teaspoon vanilla
⅛ teaspoon salt
⅛ teaspoon ground nutmeg (optional)
4 cups ½-inch cinnamon or cinnamon-raisin bread cubes
   (about 6 bread slices)
1 tablespoon margarine or butter, melted

1. Combine milk, egg substitute, sugar, vanilla, salt and nutmeg, if desired, in medium bowl; mix well. Add bread; mix until well moistened. Let stand at room temperature 15 minutes.

2. Preheat oven to 350°F. Line 12 medium-size muffin cups with paper liners. Spoon bread mixture evenly into prepared cups; drizzle evenly with margarine.

3. Bake 30 to 35 minutes or until snacks are puffed and golden brown. Remove to wire rack to cool completely.

Note: Snacks will puff up in the oven and fall slightly upon cooling.

Quick No-Bake Brownies

Makes 24 brownies

1 cup finely chopped nuts, divided
2 (1-ounce) squares unsweetened chocolate
1 (14-ounce) can EAGLE BRAND® Sweetened Condensed Milk
   (NOT evaporated milk)
2 to 2½ cups vanilla wafer crumbs (about 48 to 60 wafers)

1. Grease 9-inch square pan with butter. Sprinkle ¼ cup nuts evenly over bottom of pan. In heavy saucepan over low heat, melt chocolate with Eagle Brand. Cook and stir until mixture thickens, about 10 minutes.

2. Remove from heat; stir in crumbs and ½ cup nuts. Spread evenly in prepared pan.

3. Top with remaining ¼ cup nuts. Chill 4 hours or until firm. Cut into squares. Store loosely covered at room temperature.

Prep Time: 15 minutes
Chill Time: 4 hours

Bread Pudding Snacks

goodies **to go**

Dipped, Drizzled & Decorated Pretzels

Makes about 2 dozen pretzels

1 bag chocolate or flavored chips (choose semisweet, bittersweet, milk chocolate, green mint, white chocolate, butterscotch, peanut butter or combination)
1 bag pretzel rods
Assorted toppings: jimmies, sprinkles, chopped nuts, coconut, toasted coconut, cookie crumbs, colored sugars (optional)

1. Place chips in microwavable bowl. (Be sure bowl and utensils are completely dry.) Cover with plastic wrap and turn back one corner to vent. Microwave at HIGH for 1 minute; stir. Return to microwave and continue cooking in 30-second intervals until chips are completely melted. Check and stir frequently.

2. Dip one half of each pretzel rod into melted chocolate and decorate, if desired. Roll coated end of several pretzels in toppings. Drizzle others with contrasting color/flavor melted chips. (Drizzle melted chocolate out of spoon while rotating pretzel, to get even coverage.)

3. Place decorated pretzels on cooling rack; set over baking sheet lined with waxed-paper. Let coating harden completely. Do not refrigerate.

Walnut-Granola Clusters

Makes 5 dozen

¼ cup butter
1 (10½-ounce) package miniature marshmallows
½ teaspoon ground cinnamon
3 cups rolled oats
2 cups chopped California walnuts
1 cup flaked coconut
2 (1-ounce) squares semi-sweet chocolate

Microwave butter in large microwavable mixing bowl at HIGH (100% power) 40 seconds or until melted. Stir in marshmallows and cinnamon. Microwave 1½ minutes or until melted, stirring halfway through cooking time. Quickly stir in oats, walnuts and coconut. With wet hands, form mixture into small balls and place on wax paper-lined baking sheets.

Microwave chocolate in glass measuring cup at HIGH 2½ minutes or until melted; stir. Lightly drizzle chocolate over clusters. May be stored at room temperature, uncovered, 4 to 5 days.

*Favorite recipe from **Walnut Marketing Board***

Dipped, Drizzled & Decorated Pretzels

Mini Cheesecakes

Makes 2 dozen mini cheesecakes

> **1½ cups graham cracker or chocolate wafer crumbs**
> **¼ cup sugar**
> **¼ cup (½ stick) butter or margarine, melted**
> **3 (8-ounce) packages cream cheese, softened**
> **1 (14-ounce) can EAGLE BRAND® Sweetened Condensed Milk (NOT evaporated milk)**
> **3 eggs**
> **2 teaspoons vanilla extract**

1. Preheat oven to 300°F. In small mixing bowl, combine crumbs, sugar and butter; press equal portions firmly on bottoms of 24 lightly greased or paper-lined muffin cups.

2. In large mixing bowl, beat cream cheese until fluffy. Gradually beat in Eagle Brand until smooth. Add eggs and vanilla; mix well. Spoon equal amounts of mixture (about 3 tablespoons) into prepared cups. Bake 20 minutes or until cakes spring back when lightly touched. Cool.* Chill. Garnish as desired. Refrigerate leftovers.

*If greased muffin cups are used, cool baked cheesecakes. Freeze 15 minutes; remove with narrow spatula. Proceed as directed above.

Prep Time: 20 minutes
Bake Time: 20 minutes

Chocolate Mini Cheesecakes: Melt 1 cup (6 ounces) semi-sweet chocolate chips; mix into batter. Proceed as directed above, baking 20 to 25 minutes.

On-the-Go Guide

To soften cream cheese quickly, remove it from its wrapper and place in a medium microwavable bowl. Microwave at MEDIUM (50% power) 15 to 20 seconds or until slightly softened.

Mini Cheesecakes

out-of-the-
lunch box ideas

Cinnamon Apple Chips

Makes about 40 chips

2 cups unsweetened apple juice
1 cinnamon stick
2 Washington Red Delicious apples

1. In large skillet or saucepan, combine apple juice and cinnamon stick; bring to a low boil while preparing apples.

2. With paring knife, slice off ½ inch from tops and bottoms of apples and discard (or eat). Stand apples on either cut end; cut crosswise into ⅛-inch-thick slices, rotating apple as necessary to cut even slices.

3. Drop slices into boiling juice; cook 4 to 5 minutes or until slices appear translucent and lightly golden. Meanwhile, preheat oven to 250°F.

4. With slotted spatula, remove apple slices from juice and pat dry. Arrange slices on wire racks, being sure none overlap. Place racks on middle shelf in oven; bake 30 to 40 minutes until slices are lightly browned and almost dry to touch. Let chips cool on racks completely before storing in airtight container.

Tip: There is no need to core apples because boiling in juice for several minutes softens core and removes seeds.

*Favorite recipe from **Washington Apple Commission***

Cinnamon Apple Chips

Sweet Treat Tortillas

Makes 6 servings

> **4 (7- to 8-inch) flour tortillas**
> **4 ounces Neufchâtel cheese, softened**
> **¼ cup strawberry or other flavor spreadable fruit or preserves**
> **1 medium banana, peeled and chopped**

1. Spread each tortilla with 1 ounce Neufchâtel cheese and 1 tablespoon spreadable fruit; top with ¼ of the banana.

2. Roll up tortillas; cut crosswise into thirds.

More Sweet Treats: Substitute your favorite chopped fruit for banana.

Cinnamon-Spice Treats: Omit spreadable fruit and banana. Mix small amounts of sugar, ground cinnamon and nutmeg into Neufchâtel cheese; spread evenly onto tortillas. Sprinkle lightly with desired amount of chopped pecans or walnuts. Top with chopped fruit, if desired; roll up. Cut crosswise into thirds.

Pizza Soup

Makes 4 servings

> **2 cans (10¾ ounces each) condensed tomato soup**
> **¾ teaspoon garlic powder**
> **½ teaspoon dried oregano leaves**
> **¾ cup uncooked tiny pasta shells (¼-inch)**
> **1 cup shredded quick-melting mozzarella cheese**
> **1 cup *French's*® French Fried Onions**

1. Combine soup, *2 soup cans of water,* garlic powder and oregano in small saucepan. Bring to boiling over medium-high heat.

2. Add pasta. Cook 8 minutes or until pasta is tender.

3. Stir in cheese. Cook until cheese melts. Sprinkle with French Fried Onions.

Prep Time: 5 minutes
Cook Time: 10 minutes

Sweet Treat Tortillas

Confetti Tuna in Celery Sticks

Makes 10 to 12 servings

> 1 (3-ounce) pouch of STARKIST® Premium Albacore or Chunk
>   Light Tuna
> ½ cup shredded red or green cabbage
> ½ cup shredded carrot
> ¼ cup shredded yellow squash or zucchini
> 3 tablespoons reduced-calorie cream cheese, softened
> 1 tablespoon plain low-fat yogurt
> ½ teaspoon dried basil, crushed
>   Salt and pepper to taste
> 10 to 12 (4-inch) celery sticks, with leaves if desired

1. In a small bowl toss together tuna, cabbage, carrot and squash.

2. Stir in cream cheese, yogurt and basil. Add salt and pepper to taste.

3. With small spatula spread mixture evenly into celery sticks.

Prep Time: 20 minutes

Chocolate & Fruit Snack Mix

Makes about 11 cups

> ½ cup (1 stick) butter or margarine
> 2 tablespoons sugar
> 1 tablespoon HERSHEY'S Cocoa or HERSHEY'S Dutch
>   Processed Cocoa
> ½ teaspoon ground cinnamon
> 3 cups bite-size crisp rice squares cereal
> 3 cups bite-size crisp wheat squares cereal
> 2 cups toasted oat cereal rings
> 1 cup cashews
> 1½ cups (6-ounce package) dried fruit bits
> 1 cup HERSHEY'S Semi-Sweet Chocolate Chips

1. Place butter in 4-quart microwave-safe bowl. Microwave at HIGH
(100%) 1 minute or until melted; stir in sugar, cocoa and cinnamon.
Add cereals and cashews; stir until evenly coated. Microwave at HIGH
3 minutes, stirring after each minute; stir in dried fruit. Microwave at HIGH
3 minutes, stirring after each minute.

2. Cool completely; stir in chocolate chips. Store in tightly covered
container in cool, dry place.

Confetti Tuna in Celery Sticks

Cinnamon Raisin Roll-Ups

Makes 4 servings

4 ounces reduced-fat cream cheese, softened
½ cup shredded carrot
¼ cup golden or regular raisins
1 tablespoon honey
¼ teaspoon ground cinnamon
4 (7- to 8-inch) whole wheat or regular flour tortillas
8 thin apple wedges (optional)

1. Combine cream cheese, carrot, raisins, honey and cinnamon in small bowl; mix well.

2. Spread tortillas evenly with cream cheese mixture, leaving ½-inch border around edge of each tortilla. Place 2 apple wedges down center of each tortilla; roll up. Wrap in plastic wrap. Refrigerate until ready to serve or pack in lunch box.

Cook's Tip: For extra convenience, prepare roll-ups the night before. In the morning, pack roll-up in lunch box along with a frozen juice box. The juice box will be thawed by lunchtime and will keep the snack cold in the meantime!

Cranberry Gorp

Makes 20 servings

¼ cup unsalted butter
¼ cup packed light brown sugar
1 tablespoon maple syrup
1 teaspoon curry powder
½ teaspoon ground cinnamon
1½ cups dried cranberries
1½ cups coarsely chopped walnuts and/or slivered almonds
1½ cups lightly salted pretzel nuggets

1. Preheat oven to 300°F. Grease 15×10-inch jelly-roll pan. Combine butter, brown sugar and maple syrup in large saucepan; heat over medium heat until butter is melted. Stir in curry powder and cinnamon. Add cranberries, walnuts and pretzels; stir to combine.

2. Spread mixture on prepared pan. Bake 15 minutes or until mixture is crunchy and light brown.

Cinnamon Raisin Roll-Ups

Quick & Easy Meatball Soup

Makes 4 to 6 servings

> 1 package (15 to 18 ounces) frozen Italian sausage meatballs without sauce
> 2 cans (about 14 ounces each) Italian-style stewed tomatoes
> 2 cans (about 14 ounces each) beef broth
> 1 can (about 14 ounces) mixed vegetables
> ½ cup uncooked rotini or small macaroni
> ½ teaspoon dried oregano leaves

1. Thaw meatballs in microwave oven according to package directions.

2. Place remaining ingredients in large saucepan. Add meatballs. Bring to a boil. Reduce heat; cover and simmer 15 minutes or until pasta is tender.

Kids' Wrap

Makes 2 servings

> 4 teaspoons Dijon honey mustard
> 2 (8-inch) fat-free flour tortillas
> 2 slices reduced-fat American cheese, torn into halves
> 4 ounces fat-free oven-roasted turkey breast
> ½ cup shredded carrots (about 1 medium)
> 3 romaine lettuce leaves, washed and torn into bite-size pieces

1. Spread 2 teaspoons mustard evenly over one tortilla.

2. Top with 2 cheese halves, half of turkey, half of shredded carrots and half of torn lettuce.

3. Roll up tortilla and cut in half. Repeat with remaining ingredients for second wrap.

Quick & Easy Meatball Soup

Rainbow Spirals

Makes 4 to 6 servings

4 (10-inch) flour tortillas (assorted flavors and colors)
4 tablespoons *French's*® Mustard (any flavor)
½ pound (about 8 slices) thinly sliced deli roast beef, bologna or turkey
8 slices American, provolone or Muenster cheese
Fancy Party Toothpicks

1. Spread each tortilla with *1 tablespoon* mustard. Layer with meat and cheeses dividing evenly.

2. Roll up jelly-roll style; secure with toothpicks and cut into thirds. Arrange on platter.

Prep Time: 10 minutes

Spicy, Fruity Popcorn Mix

Makes 7 to 8 cups

4 cups lightly salted popcorn
2 cups corn cereal squares
1½ cups dried pineapple wedges
1 package (6 ounces) dried fruit bits
Butter-flavored nonstick cooking spray
1 tablespoon ground cinnamon
1 cup yogurt-covered raisins

1. Preheat oven to 350°F. Combine popcorn, cereal, pineapple and fruit bits in large bowl; mix lightly. Transfer to 15×10-inch jelly-roll pan. Spray mixture generously with cooking spray.

2. Combine sugar and cinnamon in small bowl. Sprinkle ½ of the sugar mixture over popcorn mixture; toss lightly to coat. Spray mixture again with additional cooking spray. Add remaining sugar mixture; mix lightly.

3. Bake snack mix 10 minutes, stirring after 5 minutes. Cool completely in pan on wire rack. Add raisins; mix lightly.

Rainbow Spirals

Best Ever Hero Sandwiches

Makes 4 servings

> ¼ cup Hot & Spicy Mustard (recipe follows)
> 4 (6-inch) hoagie rolls or Kaiser rolls, split
> 4 ounces sliced salami
> 4 ounces sliced smoked ham
> 4 ounces sliced provolone cheese
> 1 large tomato, sliced
> 4 large romaine lettuce leaves

1. Spread mustard evenly over bottom half of each roll.

2. Layer salami, ham, cheese, tomato and lettuce evenly on bottom half of each roll; top with top halves of rolls.

Hot & Spicy Mustard

Makes about 1 cup

> ¼ cup water
> ¼ cup whole yellow mustard seeds
> ¼ cup honey
> 3 tablespoons cider vinegar
> 2 tablespoons ground mustard
> 1 teaspoon salt
> ⅛ teaspoon ground cloves

1. Place water in small saucepan. Bring to a boil over high heat. Add mustard seeds. Cover saucepan; remove from heat. Let stand 1 hour or until liquid is absorbed.

2. Combine mustard seeds, honey, vinegar, ground mustard, salt and cloves in food processor; process using on/off pulsing action until mixture is thickened and seeds are coarsely chopped, scraping down side of work bowl occasionally. Refrigerate at least 1 day before serving. Store in airtight container in refrigerator up to 3 weeks.

Best Ever Hero Sandwich

Cucumber-Dill Dip

Makes about 2 cups dip

> 1 cucumber, peeled, seeded and finely chopped
> Salt
> 6 green onions, white parts only, chopped
> 1 package (3 ounces) reduced-fat cream cheese
> 1 cup plain yogurt
> 2 tablespoons fresh dill *or* 1 tablespoon dried dill weed
> Fresh dill sprigs

1. Lightly salt cucumber in small bowl; toss. Refrigerate 1 hour. Drain cucumber; dry on paper towels. Return cucumbers to bowl and add onions. Set aside.

2. Place cream cheese, yogurt and dill in food processor or blender; process until smooth. Stir into cucumber mixture. Cover; refrigerate 1 hour. Spoon dip into individual plastic cups with lids or glass bowl; garnish with fresh dill sprigs, if desired. Serve with vegetables, if desired.

Smoked Turkey Tortilla Roll-Ups

Makes 4 servings

> 4 (10-inch) flour tortillas
> 4 tablespoons *French's*® Sweet & Tangy Honey Mustard
> ½ pound sliced smoked turkey or ham
> 1 cup shredded lettuce
> 1 cup chopped tomatoes

1. Spread each flour tortilla with *1 tablespoon* mustard. Top with 2 slices turkey and ¼ cup *each* lettuce and tomatoes.

2. Roll up jelly-roll style. Wrap in plastic wrap; chill. Cut in half to serve.

Prep Time: 10 minutes

Cucumber-Dill Dip

Peanut Pitas

Makes 8 servings

> 1 package (8 ounces) small pita breads, cut crosswise in half
> 16 teaspoons reduced-fat peanut butter
> 16 teaspoons strawberry spreadable fruit
> 1 large banana, peeled and thinly sliced (about 48 slices)

1. Spread inside of each pita half with 1 teaspoon each peanut butter and spreadable fruit.

2. Fill pita halves evenly with banana slices. Serve immediately.

Honey Bees: Substitute honey for spreadable fruit.

Jolly Jellies: Substitute any flavor jelly for spreadable fruit and thin apple slices for banana slices.

P. B. Crunchers: Substitute reduced-fat mayonnaise for spreadable fruit and celery slices for banana slices.

On-the-Go Guide

Home-packed lunches can get boring for both kids and grownups. This recipe can help put a bit of pizzazz into portable lunch fare and provide some inspiration for thinking outside the box when it comes to midday meals.

Peanut Pitas

movable feasts

Golden Chicken Nuggets

Makes 4 servings

> 1 pound boneless skinless chicken, cut into 1½-inch pieces
> ¼ cup *French's®* Sweet & Tangy Honey Mustard
> 2 cups *French's®* French Fried Onions, finely crushed

1. Preheat oven to 400°F. Toss chicken with mustard in medium bowl.

2. Place French Fried Onions into resealable plastic food storage bag. Toss chicken in onions, a few pieces at a time, pressing gently to adhere.

3. Place nuggets in shallow baking pan. Bake 15 minutes or until chicken is no longer pink in center. Serve with additional honey mustard.

Prep Time: 5 minutes
Cook Time: 15 minutes

Golden Chicken Nuggets

Kids' Quesadillas

Makes 4 servings

>   8 slices American cheese
>   8 (10-inch) flour tortillas
>   6 tablespoons *French's*® Sweet & Tangy Honey Mustard
>   ½ pound thinly sliced deli turkey
>   2 tablespoons melted butter
>   ¼ teaspoon paprika

1. To prepare 1 quesadilla, arrange 2 slices of cheese on 1 tortilla. Top with one-fourth of the turkey. Spread with *1½ tablespoons* mustard, then top with another tortilla. Prepare 3 more quesadillas with remaining ingredients.

2. Combine butter and paprika. Brush one side of tortilla with butter mixture. Preheat 12-inch nonstick skillet over medium-high heat. Arrange tortilla butter side down and cook 2 minutes. Brush tortilla with butter mixture and turn over. Cook 1½ minutes or until golden brown. Repeat with remaining three quesadillas.

3. Slice into wedges before serving.

Prep Time: 5 minutes
Cook Time: 15 minutes

On-the-Go Guide

For most families, evenings are as hectic as mornings, with sports practice, PTA meetings, music lessons and more. These handy hand-held quesadillas are easy to heat, grab and go—no need for tableware.

Kids' Quesadillas

Lox and Cheese Mini Pizzas

Makes 20 mini pizzas (20 servings)

1 can (10 ounces) refrigerated pizza crust dough
4 ounces reduced-fat cream cheese
2 tablespoons finely chopped red onion
1 tablespoon lemon juice
2 teaspoons grated fresh lemon peel
1½ teaspoons olive oil
4 ounces thinly sliced lox or smoked salmon
Black pepper
1 tablespoon small capers, 2 teaspoons snipped fresh chives
or **20 tiny sprigs fresh dill, for garnish**

1. Prepare New York-Style Pizza Crust as directed through step 1. Preheat oven to 500°F. Lightly grease 2 large baking sheets.

2. Combine cheese, onion, juice and peel in small bowl; set aside.

3. Roll out dough into 10-inch log on lightly floured surface. Cut log into 20 (½-inch-thick) slices. Pat slices into 2¼- to 2½-inch discs. Place slightly apart on prepared baking sheets. Pierce discs several times with fork; brush evenly with oil. Bake, 1 sheet at a time, 6 minutes or until light golden. Transfer to wire rack to cool slightly.

4. Spoon about 1 teaspoon cream cheese mixture onto center of each warm crust. Spread over surface, leaving ¼-inch border. Cut lox into 2-inch pieces. Place over cream cheese. Sprinkle with pepper. Garnish each pizza as desired.

Note: To prepare these mini pizzas in advance, let the baked crusts cool completely on wire racks after being removed from the oven. Store the crusts in an airtight container at room temperature for up to 1 day.

Lox and Cheese Mini Pizza

movable feasts

Buffalo-Style Wraps

Makes 4 servings

⅔ cup *Frank's® RedHot®* Original Cayenne Pepper Sauce, divided
4 boneless skinless chicken breast halves
¼ cup blue cheese salad dressing
1 cup shredded lettuce
1 cup (4 ounces) shredded Monterey Jack cheese
4 (10-inch) flour tortillas, heated

1. Combine ⅓ cup *Frank's RedHot* Sauce and *1 tablespoon oil* in resealable plastic food storage bag. Add chicken. Seal bag; toss to coat evenly. Marinate in refrigerator 30 minutes or overnight.

2. Broil or grill chicken 10 to 15 minutes or until no longer pink in center. Slice chicken into long thin strips. In bowl, toss chicken with remaining ⅓ cup *Frank's RedHot* Sauce and dressing.

3. Arrange chicken, lettuce and cheese down center of tortillas, dividing evenly. Fold bottom third of each tortilla over filling; fold sides towards center. Tightly roll up to secure filling. Cut in half to serve.

Prep Time: 10 minutes
Cook Time: 10 minutes

Campbell's® Cheesesteak Pockets

Makes 4 sandwiches

1 tablespoon vegetable oil
1 medium onion, sliced (about ½ cup)
1 package (14 ounces) frozen beef or chicken sandwich steaks, cut into 8 pieces
1 can (10¾ ounces) CAMPBELL'S® Condensed Cheddar Cheese Soup
1 jar (about 4½ ounces) sliced mushrooms, drained
4 pita breads (6-inch), cut in half, forming two pockets each

1. In medium skillet over medium-high heat, heat oil. Add onion and cook until tender. Add sandwich steaks and cook 5 minutes or until browned, stirring often. Pour off fat.

2. Add soup and mushrooms. Heat to a boil. Reduce heat to low and heat through. Spoon meat mixture into pita halves.

Prep/Cook Time: 15 minutes

Buffalo-Style Wraps

Pizza Turnovers

Makes 6 servings

  5 ounces reduced-fat Italian bulk turkey sausage (mild)
  ½ cup pizza sauce
  1 (10-ounce) package refrigerated pizza dough
  ⅓ cup shredded reduced-fat Italian blend cheese

1. Preheat oven to 425°F. Cook sausage in nonstick saucepan until browned, stirring with spoon to break up meat. Drain off fat. Stir in pizza sauce. Cook until hot.

2. Spray baking sheet with nonstick olive oil cooking spray. Unroll pizza dough onto baking sheet. Pat into 12×8-inch rectangle. Cut into six 4×4-inch squares. Divide sausage mixture evenly among squares. Sprinkle with cheese. Lift one corner of each square and fold dough over filling to opposite corner, making a triangle. Press edges with tines of fork to seal.

3. Bake 11 to 13 minutes or until golden brown. Serve immediately or follow directions for freezing and reheating.

On-the-Go Guide

To freeze turnovers, remove to wire rack to cool 30 minutes. Individually wrap in plastic wrap, place in freezer container or plastic freezer bag and freeze. To reheat turnovers, preheat oven to 400°F. Unwrap turnovers. Place in ungreased baking pan. Cover loosely with foil. Bake 18 to 22 minutes or until hot. Or, place one turnover on a paper towel-lined microwavable plate. Heat on DEFROST (30% power) 3 to 3½ minutes or until hot, turning once.

Pizza Turnovers

movable **feasts**

5-Minute Heat and Go Soup

Makes 3½ cups (4 servings)

> 1 can (16 ounces) low-sodium navy beans, rinsed and drained
> 1 can (14½ ounces) diced tomatoes with green peppers and onions
> 1 cup water
> 1½ teaspoons dried basil leaves
> ½ teaspoon sugar
> ½ teaspoon low-sodium chicken bouillon granules
> 2 teaspoons extra-virgin olive oil

1. Place all ingredients, except oil, in medium saucepan. Bring to a boil over high heat. Reduce heat and simmer 5 minutes, uncovered. Remove from heat, stir in oil.

2. To transport, place hot soup in vacuum flask or allow to cool and place in plastic container. Reheat in microwave when needed.

Colorful Kabobs

Makes 10 kabobs

> 30 cocktail-size smoked sausages
> 10 to 20 cherry or grape tomatoes
> 10 to 20 large pimiento-stuffed green olives
> 2 yellow bell peppers, cut into 1-inch squares
> ¼ cup butter or margarine, melted
> Lemon juice (optional)

1. Preheat oven to 450°F.

2. Thread 3 sausages onto 8-inch wooden skewer*, alternating with tomatoes, olives and bell peppers. Repeat on remaining nine skewers.

3. Place skewers on rack in shallow baking pan. Brush with melted butter and drizzle with lemon juice, if desired. Bake 4 to 6 minutes until hot.

Soak skewers in water 20 minutes before using to prevent them from burning.

On-the-Go Guide: For younger children, remove food from skewers and serve in a paper cup or bowl. It's still portable, but much safer.

5-Minute Heat and Go Soup

Pizza Snack Cups

Makes 10 pizza cups

> 1 can (12 ounces) refrigerated biscuits (10 biscuits)
> ½ pound ground beef
> 1 jar (14 ounces) RAGÚ® Pizza Quick® Sauce
> ½ cup shredded mozzarella cheese (about 2 ounces)

1. Preheat oven to 375°F. In muffin pan, evenly press each biscuit in bottom and up side of each cup; chill until ready to fill.

2. In 10-inch skillet, brown ground beef over medium-high heat; drain. Stir in Ragú Pizza Quick Sauce and heat through.

3. Evenly spoon beef mixture into prepared muffin cups. Bake 15 minutes. Sprinkle with cheese and bake an additional 5 minutes or until cheese is melted and biscuits are golden. Let stand 5 minutes. Gently remove pizza cups from muffin pan and serve.

Prep Time: 10 minutes
Cook Time: 25 minutes

Dizzy Dogs

Makes 8 hot dogs

> 1 package (8 breadsticks or 11 ounces) refrigerated
>   breadsticks
> 1 package (16 ounces) hot dogs
> 1 egg white
>   Sesame and/or poppy seeds
>   Mustard, ketchup and barbecue sauce (optional)

1. Preheat oven to 375°F.

2. Using 1 breadstick for each, wrap hot dogs with dough in spiral pattern. Brush breadstick dough with egg white and sprinkle with sesame and/or poppy seeds. Place on *ungreased* baking sheet.

3. Bake 12 to 15 minutes or until light golden brown. Serve with condiments for dipping, if desired.

Pizza Snack Cups

team
treats

Crispy Chocolate Footballs

Makes about 20 small footballs

   2 cups semisweet chocolate chips
   ½ cup light corn syrup
   ¼ cup butter or margarine
   7 cups crisp rice cereal
     Powdered sugar
   ¼ recipe Cookie Glaze

SUPPLIES
   Pastry bag and small writing tip

1. Line baking sheets with waxed paper; set aside.

2. Combine chocolate chips, corn syrup and butter in medium saucepan. Cook and stir over low heat until chips are melted and mixture is smooth.

3. Place cereal in large bowl. Pour chocolate mixture over cereal; stir to coat evenly.

4. Lightly butter hands. Shape about ⅓ cup cereal mixture into football shapes, each about 2×1¼ inches in size. Place on prepared baking sheets.

5. Prepare Cookie Glaze. Stir in enough additional powdered sugar to glaze to make consistency suitable for piping. Using pastry bag fitted with writing tip, pipe lines and laces onto footballs.

Note: If desired, shape mixture into 1 large football or press mixture into greased 13×9-inch baking pan and cut into squares to serve.

Cookie Glaze: Combine 4 cups powdered sugar and 4 tablespoons milk in small bowl. Stir; add 1 to 2 tablespoons more milk as needed to make medium-thick, pourable glaze.

Left to right: Football Bears (page 72) and Crispy Chocolate Footballs

Soft Pretzels

Makes 18 large pretzels

1¼ cups milk
4 to 4½ cups all-purpose flour, divided
¼ cup sugar
1 package active dry yeast
1 teaspoon baking powder
1 teaspoon garlic salt
½ cup unsalted butter, melted
2 tablespoons baking soda
Coarse salt, sesame seeds or poppy seeds

1. Heat milk in small saucepan over low heat until temperature reaches 120° to 130°F.

2. Combine 3 cups flour, sugar, yeast, baking powder and garlic salt in large bowl. Add milk and butter. Beat vigorously 2 minutes. Add remaining flour, ¼ cup at a time, until dough begins to pull away from side of bowl.

3. Turn out dough onto lightly floured surface; flatten slightly. Knead 10 minutes or until smooth and elastic, adding flour if necessary to prevent sticking.

4. Shape dough into ball. Place in large, lightly oiled bowl; turn dough over once to oil surface. Cover with towel; let rise in warm place about 30 minutes.

5. Divide dough into 18 equal pieces. Roll each piece into 22-inch-long rope on lightly oiled surface. Form rope into "U" shape. About 2 inches from each end, cross dough. Cross second time. Fold loose ends up to rounded part of "U"; press ends to seal. Turn pretzels over so that ends are on underside and reshape if necessary. Cover with towel; let rest 20 minutes.

6. Preheat oven to 400°F. Grease baking sheets or line with parchment paper. Fill large Dutch oven ¾ full with water. Bring to a boil over high heat. Add baking soda. Carefully drop pretzels, 3 at a time, into boiling water for 10 seconds. Remove with slotted spoon. Place on prepared baking sheets. Sprinkle with coarse salt, sesame seeds or poppy seeds.

7. Bake 15 minutes or until golden brown. Place on wire rack.

Soft Pretzels

Snacking Surprise Muffins

Makes 12 servings

   1½ **cups all-purpose flour**
   ½ **cup sugar**
   1 **cup fresh or frozen blueberries**
   2½ **teaspoons baking powder**
   1 **teaspoon ground cinnamon**
   ¼ **teaspoon salt**
   1 **egg, beaten**
   ⅔ **cup buttermilk**
   ¼ **cup margarine or butter, melted**
   3 **tablespoons peach preserves**

TOPPING
   1 **tablespoon sugar**
   ¼ **teaspoon ground cinnamon**

1. Preheat oven to 400°F. Line 12 medium muffin cups with paper liners; set aside.

2. Combine flour, ½ cup sugar, blueberries, baking powder, 1 teaspoon cinnamon and salt in medium bowl. Combine egg, buttermilk and margarine in small bowl. Add to flour mixture; mix just until moistened.

3. Spoon about 1 tablespoon batter into each muffin cup. Drop a scant teaspoonful of preserves into center of batter in each cup; top with remaining batter.

4. Combine 1 tablespoon sugar and ¼ teaspoon cinnamon in small bowl; sprinkle evenly over tops of batter.

5. Bake 18 to 20 minutes or until lightly browned. Remove muffins to wire rack to cool completely.

On-the-Go Guide

Active families often almost literally eat on the run. These power-packed snacks are perfect to tote along to sports practice or a workout, or when it's your family's turn to provide team snacks after the game. Portable, popular and easy to pack individually, these muffins are sure to be winners every time.

Snacking Surprise Muffins

Football Bears

Makes 12 bears

INGREDIENTS

1¼ cups water

½ cup butter

1¼ cups all-purpose flour

⅛ teaspoon salt

5 eggs

1¼ cups prepared vanilla pudding

1 package (12 ounces) butterscotch chips

3 tablespoons shortening

Powdered sugar

1 recipe Cookie Glaze (page 66)

Mini semisweet chocolate chips

Candy-coated chocolate pieces

Assorted food colorings

SUPPLIES

Parchment paper

Pastry bags, large writing tip and small writing tip

1. Bring water and butter to a boil in medium saucepan. Add flour and salt; stir until dough forms a ball. Remove from heat; beat in eggs, 1 at a time, with wooden spoon or wire whisk until dough is smooth and shiny.

2. Preheat oven to 400°F. Line baking sheet with parchment paper. Using pastry bag fitted with large writing tip, pipe dough into 3×1½-inch oval on prepared baking sheet for body. Repeat to make 11 additional ovals, spacing ovals about 2 inches apart.

3. Pipe ¾-inch rounds for heads and four ½-inch rounds for legs and arms as shown in diagram. Pipe small round at base of each head for bear's snout and 2 small dots at top of head for ears. Repeat for remaining bears.

4. Bake 10 minutes. Reduce heat to 350°F. Bake 25 to 30 minutes or until golden brown. Carefully remove bears to wire racks; cool completely.

5. Using serrated knife, slice off top of rounded stomach on each bear. Scoop out soft dough; discard. Spoon pudding evenly into stomach cavities; replace tops of stomachs. Place bears on wire rack over waxed paper.

6. Melt butterscotch chips with shortening in top of double boiler over hot water, stirring until smooth; spoon over bears, spreading to coat evenly. Refrigerate 10 minutes or until coating is firm.

7. Add enough powdered sugar to Cookie Glaze for proper piping consistency. Use small dabs of glaze to attach chocolate chips for eyes and candy pieces for noses. Remove about ¼ of glaze for decorating shirts. Tint as desired and spoon into pastry bag fitted with small writing tip; set aside.

8. Color remaining glaze as desired; spread onto fronts of bears to resemble shirts. Using frosting in pastry bag, pipe stripes and numbers on shirts to resemble football jerseys. Refrigerate until ready to serve. Refrigerate any leftovers.

On-the-Go Guide

A pastry bag is a cone-shaped bag made of canvas, plastic or plastic-lined cloth. It is open at both ends. The food to be piped is placed in the larger opening. The smaller opening can be fitted with various decorative tips.

Take-Along Snack Mix

Makes about 3½ cups

1 tablespoon butter or margarine
2 tablespoons honey
1 cup toasted oat cereal, any flavor
½ cup coarsely broken pecans
½ cup thin pretzel sticks, broken in half
½ cup raisins
1 cup "M&M's"® Chocolate Mini Baking Bits

In large heavy skillet over low heat, melt butter; add honey and stir until blended. Add cereal, nuts, pretzels and raisins, stirring until all pieces are evenly coated. Continue cooking over low heat about 10 minutes, stirring frequently. Remove from heat; immediately spread on waxed paper until cool. Add "M&M's"® Chocolate Mini Baking Bits. Store in tightly covered container.

Peanut Butter Crispy Treats

Makes about 3 dozen

4 cups toasted rice cereal
1¾ cups "M&M's"® Milk Chocolate Mini Baking Bits
4 cups mini marshmallows
½ cup creamy peanut butter
¼ cup butter or margarine
⅛ teaspoon salt

Combine cereal and "M&M's"® Milk Chocolate Mini Baking Bits in lightly greased baking pan; set aside. Melt marshmallows, peanut butter, butter and salt in heavy saucepan over low heat, stirring occasionally until mixture is smooth. Pour melted mixture over cereal mixture, tossing lightly until thoroughly coated. Gently shape into 1½-inch balls with buttered fingers. Place on waxed paper; cool at room temperature until set. Store in tightly covered container.

Variation: After cereal mixture is thoroughly coated, press lightly into greased 13×9×2-inch pan. Cool completely; cut into bars. Makes 24 bars.

Top to bottom: Take-Along Snack Mix, Peanut Butter Crispy Treats

ready when
you are

The Best Beef Stew

Makes 8 servings

- ½ cup plus 2 tablespoons all-purpose flour, divided
- 2 teaspoons salt
- 1 teaspoon black pepper
- 3 pounds beef for stew, cut into 1-inch pieces
- 1 can (16 ounces) diced tomatoes in juice, undrained
- 3 potatoes, peeled and diced
- ½ pound smoked sausage, sliced
- 1 cup chopped leek
- 1 cup chopped onion
- 4 ribs celery, sliced
- ½ cup chicken broth
- 3 cloves garlic, minced
- 1 teaspoon dried thyme leaves
- 3 tablespoons water

SLOW COOKER DIRECTIONS

1. Combine ½ cup flour, salt and pepper in resealable plastic food storage bag. Add beef; shake bag to coat beef. Place beef in slow cooker. Add remaining ingredients except remaining 2 tablespoons flour and water; stir well. Cover and cook on LOW 8 to 12 hours or on HIGH 4 to 6 hours.

2. One hour before serving, turn slow cooker to HIGH. Combine remaining 2 tablespoons flour and water in small bowl; stir until mixture becomes paste. Stir mixture into slow cooker; mix well. Cover and cook until thickened. Garnish as desired.

The Best Beef Stew

Suzie's Sloppy Joes

Makes 8 to 10 servings

>   3 pounds 90% lean ground beef
>   1 cup chopped onion
>   3 cloves garlic, minced
>   1¼ cups ketchup
>   1 cup chopped red bell pepper
>   5 tablespoons Worcestershire sauce
>   4 tablespoons brown sugar
>   3 tablespoons vinegar
>   3 tablespoons prepared mustard
>   2 teaspoons chili powder
>   Hamburger buns

SLOW COOKER DIRECTIONS

1. Brown ground beef, onion and garlic in large skillet. Drain excess fat.

2. Combine ketchup, bell pepper, Worcestershire sauce, brown sugar, vinegar, mustard and chili powder in slow cooker. Stir in beef mixture. Cover and cook on LOW 6 to 8 hours. Spoon into hamburger buns.

On-the-Go Guide

No matter what time your busy family finally sits down to dinner, slow cookers make it possible to have food on the table minutes after you walk through that door. Use healthy convenience foods such as bagged salad mixes, to quickly create a complete meal.

Suzie's Sloppy Joes

3-Cheese Chicken & Noodles

Makes 6 servings

>   3 cups chopped cooked chicken
>   1½ cups cottage cheese
>   1 can (10¾ ounces) condensed cream of chicken soup,
>   undiluted
>   1 package (8 ounces) wide egg noodles, cooked and drained
>   1 cup grated Monterey Jack cheese
>   ½ cup diced celery
>   ½ cup diced onion
>   ½ cup diced green bell pepper
>   ½ cup diced red bell pepper
>   ½ cup grated Parmesan cheese
>   ½ cup chicken broth
>   1 can (4 ounces) sliced mushrooms, drained
>   2 tablespoons butter, melted
>   ½ teaspoon dried thyme leaves

SLOW COOKER DIRECTIONS
Combine all ingredients in slow cooker. Stir to coat evenly. Cover; cook on LOW 6 to 10 hours or on HIGH 3 to 4 hours.

On-the-Go Guide

Serving a simple vegetable side dish with this recipe makes a complete and nutritious meal. If your kids balk at eating green vegetables, don't give up. Other colorful vegetables bring a lot of excellent nutrients to the table and may taste less bitter to young palates. Carrots, corn, sweet potatoes and squash are excellent choices.

3-Cheese Chicken & Noodles

Broccoli and Beef Pasta

Makes 4 servings

> 2 cups broccoli florets *or* 1 package (10 ounces) frozen
>   broccoli, thawed
> 1 onion, thinly sliced
> ½ teaspoon dried basil leaves
> ½ teaspoon dried oregano leaves
> ½ teaspoon dried thyme leaves
> 1 can (14½ ounces) Italian-style diced tomatoes, undrained
> ¾ cup beef broth
> 1 pound lean ground beef
> 2 cloves garlic, minced
> 2 tablespoons tomato paste
> 2 cups cooked rotini pasta
> 3 ounces shredded Cheddar cheese or grated Parmesan
>   cheese

SLOW COOKER DIRECTIONS

1. Layer broccoli, onion, basil, oregano, thyme, tomatoes with juice and beef broth in slow cooker. Cover; cook on LOW 2½ hours.

2. Combine beef and garlic in large nonstick skillet; cook over high heat 6 to 8 minutes or until meat is no longer pink, breaking meat apart with wooden spoon. Pour off drippings. Add beef mixture to slow cooker. Cover; cook 2 hours.

3. Stir in tomato paste. Add pasta and cheese. Cover; cook 30 minutes or until cheese melts and mixture is heated through. Sprinkle with additional shredded cheese, if desired.

Serving Suggestion: Garlic bread goes great with this dish!

Broccoli and Beef Pasta

Mile-High Enchilada Pie

Makes 4 to 6 servings

8 (6-inch) corn tortillas
1 jar (12 ounces) prepared salsa
1 can (15½ ounces) kidney beans, rinsed and drained
1 cup shredded cooked chicken
1 cup shredded Monterey Jack cheese with jalapeño peppers

SLOW COOKER DIRECTIONS
Prepare foil handles for slow cooker (see below); place in slow cooker. Place 1 tortilla on bottom of slow cooker. Top with small amount of salsa, beans, chicken and cheese. Continue layering using remaining ingredients, ending with cheese. Cover; cook on LOW 6 to 8 hours or on HIGH 3 to 4 hours. Pull out by foil handles.

Foil Handles: Tear off three 18×2-inch strips of heavy foil or use regular foil folded to double thickness. Crisscross foil strips in spoke design and place in slow cooker to make lifting of tortilla stack easier.

On-the-Go Guide

If your family prefers a different kind of meat, try cooked pork, steak or ground beef. This recipe is great to use for leftovers from the night before.

Mile-High Enchilada Pie

Turkey and Macaroni

Makes 4 to 6 servings

> 1 teaspoon vegetable oil
> 1½ pounds ground turkey
> 2 cans (10¾ ounces each) condensed tomato soup, undiluted
> 2 cups uncooked macaroni, cooked and drained
> 1 can (16 ounces) corn, drained
> ½ cup chopped onion
> 1 can (4 ounces) sliced mushrooms, drained
> 2 tablespoons ketchup
> 1 tablespoon mustard
> Salt and black pepper to taste

SLOW COOKER DIRECTIONS

Heat oil in medium skillet; cook turkey until browned. Transfer mixture to slow cooker. Add remaining ingredients to slow cooker. Stir to blend. Cover and cook on LOW 7 to 9 hours or on HIGH 3 to 4 hours.

On-the-Go Guide

Make sure to keep the lid on! The slow cooker can take as long as 30 minutes to regain heat lost when the lid is removed. Only remove the lid when instructed to do so in the recipe.

Turkey and Macaroni

Italian Beef

Makes 8 servings

1 beef rump roast (3 to 5 pounds)
1 can (14 ounces) beef broth
2 cups mild giardiniera

SLOW COOKER DIRECTIONS

1. Place rump roast in slow cooker; add beef broth and giardiniera.

2. Cover; cook on LOW 10 hours.

3. Shred beef; serve with sauce on crusty Italian rolls.

Caribbean Shrimp with Rice

Makes 4 servings

1 package (12 ounces) frozen shrimp, thawed
½ cup fat-free reduced-sodium chicken broth
1 clove garlic, minced
1 teaspoon chili powder
½ teaspoon salt
½ teaspoon dried oregano leaves
1 cup frozen peas, thawed
½ cup diced tomatoes
2 cups cooked long-grain white rice

SLOW COOKER DIRECTIONS

Combine shrimp, broth, garlic, chili powder, salt and oregano in slow cooker. Cover and cook on LOW 2 hours. Add peas and tomatoes. Cover and cook on LOW 5 minutes. Stir in rice. Cover and cook on LOW an additional 5 minutes.

Italian Beef

Mexican-Style Rice and Cheese

Makes 6 to 8 servings

> 1 can (16 ounces) Mexican-style beans
> 1 can (14½ ounces) diced tomatoes with jalapeños, undrained
> 1½ cups uncooked long-grain converted rice
> 1 large onion, finely chopped
> ½ package (4 ounces) cream cheese
> 3 cloves garlic, minced
> 2 cups (8 ounces) shredded Monterey Jack or Colby cheese, divided

SLOW COOKER DIRECTIONS

1. Mix all ingredients thoroughly except 1 cup shredded cheese. Pour mixture into well-greased slow cooker. Cover; cook on LOW 6 to 9 hours.

2. Just before serving, sprinkle with remaining 1 cup shredded cheese.

Simple Slow Cooker Pork Roast

Makes 6 servings

> 4 to 5 red potatoes, cut into bite-size pieces
> 4 carrots, cut into bite-size pieces
> 1 marinated pork loin roast (3 to 4 pounds)
> ½ cup water
> 1 package (10 ounces) frozen baby peas
> Salt
> Black pepper

SLOW COOKER DIRECTIONS

Place potatoes, carrots and pork roast in slow cooker. (If necessary, cut roast in half to fit in slow cooker.) Add water. Cover; cook on LOW 6 to 8 hours or until vegetables are tender. Add peas during last hour of cooking. Season to taste with salt and pepper.

Mexican-Style Rice and Cheese

Vegetarian Lasagna

Makes 4 to 6 servings

> 1 small eggplant, sliced into ½-inch rounds
> ½ teaspoon salt
> 2 tablespoons olive oil, divided
> 1 tablespoon butter
> ½ pound mushrooms, sliced
> 1 small onion, diced
> 1 can (26 ounces) pasta sauce
> 1 teaspoon dried basil
> 1 teaspoon dried oregano
> 2 cups part-skim ricotta cheese
> 1½ cups (6 ounces) shredded Monterey Jack cheese
> 1 cup grated Parmesan cheese, divided
> 1 package (8 ounces) whole wheat lasagna noodles, cooked and drained
> 1 medium zucchini, thinly sliced

SLOW COOKER DIRECTIONS

1. Sprinkle eggplant with salt; let sit 10 to 15 minutes. Rinse and pat dry; brush with 1 tablespoon olive oil. Brown on both sides in medium skillet over medium heat. Set aside.

2. Heat remaining 1 tablespoon olive oil and butter in same skillet over medium heat; cook and stir mushrooms and onion until softened. Stir in pasta sauce, basil and oregano. Set aside.

3. Combine ricotta cheese, Monterey Jack cheese and ½ cup Parmesan cheese in medium bowl. Set aside.

4. Spread ⅓ sauce mixture in bottom of slow cooker. Layer with ⅓ of lasagna noodles, ½ of eggplant, ½ of cheese mixture. Repeat layers once. For last layer, use final ⅓ of lasagna noodles, zucchini, final ⅓ of sauce mixture and top with remaining ½ cup Parmesan.

5. Cover; cook on LOW 6 hours. Let sit 15 to 20 minutes before serving.

acknowledgments

The publisher would like to thank the companies and organizations listed below for the use of their recipes and photographs in this publication.

Bob Evans®

Campbell Soup Company

Dole Food Company, Inc.

Eagle Brand®

Hershey Foods Corporation

© Mars, Incorporated 2004

Reckitt Benckiser Inc.

The J.M. Smucker Company

StarKist® Seafood Company

Unilever Bestfoods North America

USA Rice

Walnut Marketing Board

Washington Apple Commission

index

METRIC CONVERSION CHART

VOLUME MEASUREMENTS (dry)

1/8 teaspoon = 0.5 mL
1/4 teaspoon = 1 mL
1/2 teaspoon = 2 mL
3/4 teaspoon = 4 mL
1 teaspoon = 5 mL
1 tablespoon = 15 mL
2 tablespoons = 30 mL
1/4 cup = 60 mL
1/3 cup = 75 mL
1/2 cup = 125 mL
2/3 cup = 150 mL
3/4 cup = 175 mL
1 cup = 250 mL
2 cups = 1 pint = 500 mL
3 cups = 750 mL
4 cups = 1 quart = 1 L

VOLUME MEASUREMENTS (fluid)

1 fluid ounce (2 tablespoons) = 30 mL
4 fluid ounces (1/2 cup) = 125 mL
8 fluid ounces (1 cup) = 250 mL
12 fluid ounces (1 1/2 cups) = 375 mL
16 fluid ounces (2 cups) = 500 mL

WEIGHTS (mass)

1/2 ounce = 15 g
1 ounce = 30 g
3 ounces = 90 g
4 ounces = 120 g
8 ounces = 225 g
10 ounces = 285 g
12 ounces = 360 g
16 ounces = 1 pound = 450 g

DIMENSIONS

1/16 inch = 2 mm
1/8 inch = 3 mm
1/4 inch = 6 mm
1/2 inch = 1.5 cm
3/4 inch = 2 cm
1 inch = 2.5 cm

OVEN TEMPERATURES

250°F = 120°C
275°F = 140°C
300°F = 150°C
325°F = 160°C
350°F = 180°C
375°F = 190°C
400°F = 200°C
425°F = 220°C
450°F = 230°C

BAKING PAN SIZES

Utensil	Size in Inches/Quarts	Metric Volume	Size in Centimeters
Baking or	8×8×2	2 L	20×20×5
Cake Pan	9×9×2	2.5 L	23×23×5
(square or	12×8×2	3 L	30×20×5
rectangular)	13×9×2	3.5 L	33×23×5
Loaf Pan	8×4×3	1.5 L	20×10×7
	9×5×3	2 L	23×13×7
Round Layer	8×1½	1.2 L	20×4
Cake Pan	9×1½	1.5 L	23×4
Pie Plate	8×1¼	750 mL	20×3
	9×1¼	1 L	23×3
Baking Dish	1 quart	1 L	—
or Casserole	1½ quart	1.5 L	—
	2 quart	2 L	—